Kindle Publisning Back End

Guide To Creating A Real Business With Kindle Publishing

Argena Olivis

www.ArgenaOlivis.com

BONUS! Grab My FREE CreateSpace Book Creation Course and ACX Audiobook Creation Course

Get more exposure to your Kindle books by creating paperback books, this means more sales, more authority and leads for the back end of your business!

www.argenaolivis.com/createspaceandaudiobook

As an added bonus, you'll get my ACX Audiobook Creation Course where you'll discover how **to get an audiobook created for FREE!**

Table of Contents

Introduction

Thank you for downloading this particular book, as an author I know how easy can be to discard anyone trying to tell you how to run your business. But for those who are looking for some new ideas and guidance, this book is for you.

It's very scary, super scary, when you have all your eggs in one basket. When you put your financial future in the hands of a company. Even if you do everything right, you still never know.

If your KDP account was shut down today, do you have a backup plan? If not, you're scaring me. I don't want you to live this way. And in this book, we're going to go into how to build the back end of your business.

When I say "back end" I'm referring to making an income outside of your books. I'll give you a clue on the main way you're going to do that: email marketing.

We'll go into how to build up a series of books that will funnel readers into other products that will bring them value.

You'll discover how to build a tribe of loyal readers that will review your books and support you in anything you release.

Now don't get me wrong, I do want you to focus on what you do best: writing; but I also want you to be smart about it. By managing your time effectively, you can build a list, write, and promote your book all at the same time.

We'll go into exactly how to do that in chapter 7 when we

discuss how to build a real business.

When I say real business, I mean something that you have some control over. Building up loyal readers and fans while having them as your customers; not just Amazon's.

Why I Wrote This Book:

I wrote this book because I got scared. I started to make a pretty decent income through my books and I wanted to make sure I wasn't going to lose everything.

Although I try not to do anything wrong, I don't like my business being in the hands of someone else.

I now look at my books as a lead generator. Although they bring in a nice income, I can make way more money on the back end.

I knew I had to have a plan. I also knew that I wanted to leverage Amazon's traffic to generate leads and ultimately turn those leads into my own customers and fans.

I wrote this book because I know there are a lot of authors out there that struggle with this. Who have all their eggs in one basket, and is an account deactivation away from being broke.

I love writing, and I love helping my fellow authors. I wrote this book to save a few people from big trouble, and to help authors to increase their income.

Thanks again for investing in this book, make sure to take action on what you learn and apply it sooner than later. Without action, nothing is possible.

Chapter 1: Getting Email Addresses

I really hope you're already building a list, if so this chapter will be a review for you; you'll learn where you can get some more ideas, how to increase opt ins, and build your book business even bigger.

If you're not building a list, shame on you. I don't know what's holding you back but you better get to it. Right now!

I'm serious, this whole book will be pointless if you don't have a list.

Why Do You Need A List

You need a list so you can build a community of readers and fans around your books and your brand as a whole.

Also, in the introduction I talked about not putting all your eggs in one basket. A profitable list will help eliminate that.

An email list is the most secure asset that you'll ever have in your business. If something goes wrong, you can turn to you list and update them. If you have a sale that ends soon, you can turn to your list and let them know. If your website is down, you can let you list know.

The reason email lists are so secure is because you can back up all the email addresses you have, so even if you something happens to your email provider, you can always have those email addresses.

Email lists can also be a big deal when it comes to your books. With one email sent to responsive list, you can get lots of reviews for your books early on. You can also let them know about upcoming books so they can pre-order.

You can create an entire book launch around your book and have your readers vote for what covers they like best, and even put out review copies to get early feedback on your work.

There are so many benefits to having an email list. The most important one, in my opinion, is security. You don't want to have books as your only source of income. Most successful entrepreneurs diversify, which eliminates risks and gives you and your family more peace of mind.

How Much Will It Cost Me

If you're worried about how much an email list will cost you. You're asking the wrong question. You should be asking how much it will make you.

Cost will ultimately depend on the email software you use. There are some software that you can use for free until you get so many subscribers, then you start paying.

I personally stay clear of the free ones because I don't like how many rules they have. Some of the free ones have rules against certain things like affiliate links and product promotion.

I don't know about you, but I like to have as much freedom as possible in my business.

I use a popular service called Aweber. It's very affordable for when you're first getting started.

To get **step by step instructions for beginners** visit http://www.argenaolivis.com/email-marketing-101/ for a full tutorial on how to get started with Aweber.

There are other services too, that I've heard great things about, such as: GetResponse, Ontraport, and Infusionsoft, etc.

So now you understand the importance of an email list. Take action now before we get into the next section of chapter 1. You're going to need your list set up so we can create our opt in offer.

Create Your Opt In Offer

Your opt in offer is what you'll give your subscribers for free in exchange for their contact information; such as a name or email address.

An opt in offer for an author can be a many things. I'm going to go into the most popular offers that convert the best.

Remember to test; if you see your opt in offer is working, that's great, but you should still test to see if another offer converts better. If your opt in offer isn't converting, create a new one as soon as possible.

You'll know if it's converting if people are visiting your opt in form and opting in to your list. If people are visiting your form and not opting in, then you need to tweak or change the offer all together.

Not everyone will want what you have to offer. Others just don't like being on email lists. That's why you have to treat your email list well and provide them with massive value.

They are most likely already getting emails from your competitors, so you have to stand out by **offering more value on a more consistent basis.**

Keep in mind that this is the first impression you have on your readers outside of your book. So make the opt in offer really good.

Types of opt in offers for authors can include, but are not limited to:

- bonus chapter (s)

- audiobook

- video/mini course

- report

- check list

- free book

- printable(s)

Bonus Chapter

Creating a bonus chapter for your audience is a wonderful idea and I'm sure that it will convert well for both nonfiction and fiction authors. Make the bonus chapter something enticing, **make it something your readers will not want to miss out on.**

Create curiosity and excitement when offering this opt in offer. Put yourself in the reader's shoes and think about what readers will want to learn about next if you're nonfiction. If you're fiction, think of a scene that readers will want to read about, or a continuation of a scene.

You can do more than one bonus chapter too. You don't have to tell your readers about the extra bonus chapter, you can put in an auto responder message so they'll get it the next day or within the next few days.

There's nothing more that customers love than surprise bonuses that are free and add value to their lives. They're weren't expecting it, and it helps build trust and authority. Many authors aren't using surprise bonuses, so it's a way for you to stick out while amazing your readers.

Delivery: Deliver your bonus chapter directly in the email; or create a PDF and give your subscribers a link to it.

Depending how fancy you are, if you have a website, you can create a free membership site (using the s2member plugin on WordPress), and make it so your readers get a username and password upon opting in to your list. From there, they'll be able to log in to their account and get access to the bonus chapter.

Audiobook

Readers will love this. Instead of giving them something else to read, give them something that they can listen to at their own leisure.

Most customers will read through the book and get the audiobook and listen to the book on a separate occasion.

Some may buy your book just to get the free audiobook version.

You can create an audiobook for fairly cheap by yourself, or you can outsource it. Outsourcing it will definitely save you time, but it can be expensive.

If you decide to outsource it, consider using a service such as odesk.com. You should be able to find someone quality there to create you audiobook. All you have to do is create a job posting.

Before hiring anyone, make sure to look at the feedback they received on Odesk, and ask them a few important questions you may want to know before you hire them for the project.

If you decide to do this yourself, keep in mind that you don't need fancy and expensive equipment to get quality sound. You can buy an affordable usb microphone or you can use headphones that have a microphone built in.

You can use a service such as Free Conference Call, Soundcloud, Audacity, or other places to record audio. Record your book, and download the file as an mp3 so it can be delivered to your customers.

Video/Mini Course

This works especially for nonfiction books. I use this for a lot of my opt in offers. It converts really well. Although your readers love to read, sometimes it's nice to learn how to do something hands on.

The only way I can see this working for a fiction is you creating a slideshow of what your characters look like, or you actually have people acting out a scene from your book. Or you can do a video about you, the author. Get to know your readers by telling them how you came up with the stories and what inspired you to write what you did.

You don't need a fancy camera to create video. The quality of most smart phones will suffice. Keep in mind that you don't have to be in the video. You can easily record your computer screen and create a little mini course or instructional video.

If you don't have a smart phone and you want to record yourself, use a digital camera. You can find quality digital cameras for very cheap these days. Try to record your video using natural light; somewhere near a window (so it's best to record during the day).

Also, make an outline before you start recording. Write down points you want to touch on in the video; and it will flow more smoothly. You can always edit it later.

If you want to create a mini course, you can create a PowerPoint Presentation on what you will be covering before you start creating your video.

To record your screen, use tools such as Jing or Screen-Cast-O-Matic. They're both free and or very low cost ways to capture your screen and your audio at the same time. It's also easy to download files to your computer so you can send them to your subscribers.

If you do webinars, you can use a replay as your "free video". If they really like your replay, your readers will look forward to your next webinar if you put another one on.

If I'm giving away a free video to my subscribers, I usually record my screen using Screen-Cast-O-Matic and then download the video to my computer, edit it using Windows Live Movie Maker, then upload it to YouTube and set it as "unlisted".

When you create an unlisted video on YouTube, only people with that link are allowed access to it. Yes, it can be shared if people want to break the rules, but who cares you can't worry about that; it's a free video anyways so nothing lost.

Report

A report is great for nonfiction authors too. A report allows you to send your reader information that they can take action on and get immediate results with.

Reports don't' have to be long, about 6+ pages. They just need to benefit the reader and help them do something or figure something out.

If you decide to go with a report, make sure it's really good and that your audience will actually want to read it.

Make the title of the report enticing so readers want to opt in and subscribe to your list. Tell the reader what results they will receive if they use the strategies and tips in the report.

Outline the benefits to reading the report, and pay close attention to your headlines. Copywriting plays a big role in getting people to opt in and read your stuff.

When I'm searching for headlines, I usually turn to magazines because they have some great ideas for headlines.

Keep in mind that your reader may not feel like reading something else, they may want something more personal such as a video or audiobook. But this strategy still works.

It all depends on your target market. Also, make sure your report is directly related to what your book is about.

Make sure, just like your books, your report is edited and very appealing to the eye. Try to spice it up by adding colored text, leaving a lot of white space, bolding important points, and having a clear action statement at the end.

Checklist

I use checklists for some of my opt in offers. I depends on your target market and what you're trying to teach them.

I think checklists are every helpful if done right.

You create a checklist by simply using a Microsoft Word document or pdf and have your readers download it to their computers after opting in.

You can copy and paste boxes for your check boxes from creativestable.com by clicking here.

Make sure the checklist is printable; it'll be more convenient for your subscribers.

Your checklist should be a list of items that your readers will need to get started, a list of tasks they need to complete, or a list of action steps to take.

Free Book

Giving away a free book is a great idea for fiction offers. You can give away the next book in the series to pull readers in and then have the third book for sale.

A free book can also work for nonfiction writers. You can give away a related eBook that may go more in depth about how to do something, or you can just stick to the report.

Depending on your budget and how much time you have, you can also give away paperback books. Think about how much this will help your audience connect with you if something is sent to their door.

Most big authors that do this just have the readers pay shipping. Be sure to give away the eBook version for free though; you don't want to upset your readers by not giving them something completely free like you promised.

Creating an eBook is simple, you already know how to do

it. It's just alike Kindle book, but you'll just be sending the PDF or Document to your subscribers.

Keep in mind that the book should be something that your readers will want.

Printables

Printables have been an effective opt in offer for one of my lists too. Printables can work for target markets that are more creative.

You can have a collection of printables that include:

- checklists

- templates

- scripts

- tips

- etc.

Usually when giving away printables, you do so in a bundle. It's a really fun and creative way to help others and can definitely be used for most nonfiction books.

The great thing about printables is that it makes what you are teaching more hands on and gets the subscriber involved.

Outsourcing Your Opt In Offer

As a writer, you know what your main focus should be. Writing new books and coming up with new ideas. So you may not have the time or the patience to put together an opt in offer.

That's why it's great that we have the internet; where we

can hire people to do the things that need to be done, but you don't necessarily have the time or passion to do.

Don't think that you have to do everything yourself in this business, you may actually have some books ghostwritten; so you may be already very fond of outsourcing.

You can have your opt in offer created by someone on an outsourcing service such as Odesk. Just post the job and the job description and you'll get applicants that are eager to start creating your offer.

Make sure to be careful when selecting the right person to do the job. Look at their feedback rating and see if they have experience in that particular area.

The only type of thing I wouldn't outsource are videos and mini courses. When your reader receives the video, they'll be expecting that it was created by the author. Plus, videos help you connect better with your readers.

But outsourcing bonus chapters, audiobooks, reports, books, printables, and checklists are a great idea. Go for it, save yourself some time and keep working on the things that matter most as a business owner.

Odesk is not the only place to get things done. You can also go with Elance.com, Fiverr.com, and other outsourcing services. I personally use Odesk and have had great experiences, that's why I recommend them.

Picture of Your Opt In Offer

If you want people to opt in, you want to make sure you have an image of what they'll be receiving.

Opt in offers that have pictures to describe them convert much better than just plain text. You can get an image of your offer created or you can simply take a screen shot of it and doctor it up to make it look more appealing.

If you're giving away a free book, this will be easy. Just have an image of the book cover. For things like your course, have an image of the video or get a template of something that looks like a DVD and put the title of the video on there.

You can get very creative with this process. If you're going to get fancy, make sure to outsource the design. Fiverr.com would be great for this type of work.

If you decide you want to just take a screen shot and doctor it up, use free editing tools like www.picmokey.com or www.canva.com.

Where Should Your Opt In Offer Go?

Put it at the very beginning of your book, right after the title page. And at the very end of your book.

You can mention it inside your book, but don't get too crazy with this. If you do mention it throughout the book make sure it's relevant to what you're talking about at the particular moment.

You can get more advanced with putting offers in the front and back of your book, but we'll get more into that in Chapter 5: Separate Lists/Segmentation.

The Takeaway

Okay, so now you know that you need an email list. You should have already got started and signed up for an email marketing software where you can keep your subscriber's emails stored and send messages to your readers.

Having a list will create more security in your business, and also make you more money in the long run if you create more value.

You should have also created your opt in offer. Pick one that works well for your target market and make sure it's somehow related to your book(s).

If you don't want to create you offer, you should be getting one outsourced.

Please take action on these items before moving on the next chapter.

Chapter 2: Creating Squeeze/Landing Page

A squeeze page or landing page is a page that has only one agenda: to get the prospects email address. Or sometimes name and email address.

These days, there's so many tools that can help you create a squeeze page in just minutes. All the squeeze page tools do the same thing, but the quality may vary.

Your email marketing software most likely comes with templates or opt in boxes that you can use to create a squeeze page.

The idea here is to have a link that goes directly to an opt in page. The prospect will see an image when they go to the page. They'll also see a description, and box for their name and email address.

If the prospect wants the opt in offer, they'll go on and enter their information. If not, they'll have the option to exit the page.

Now days, they have confirmed that double opt ins increase conversions. This means on the first page the prospect will see an image and or description of what the free offer is. Then they have to click on a button to go on and enter their email address.

This helps the prospect confirm that it's really what they want, because they took and extra step to opt in; instead of just seeing a place to enter their email right away.

Squeeze Page Tools

When you're first starting out, you may not have a budget for tools such as LeadPages. They do have a great product with tested conversions for email opt ins, but it may not be affordable for the average author trying to keep their costs to a minimum.

There are also lower cost programs like Optimize Press and Landing Page Monkey. Right now I'm using Landing Page Monkey. It pretty much has the same functions as LeadPages but for a one-time fee.

Before I started using Landing Page Monkey, I was just using the link from my Aweber forms so leads can opt in right away. Click here to see an example. All of my opt ins aren't converted yet, but it's in the process.

Just to let you know, you don't need anything fancy to get subscribers. Yes, some tools may increase conversions, but you want to focus on getting something out there. Don't get held up with all these fancy tools.

Once you start really making some money and freeing up your time, you can always go back and improve your opt in forms or sign up for these programs. Right now just focus on getting something up so you can start building your back end.

Once you do create your landing page, it's time to put the opt in offer inside your book.

After your title page, have a page where you describe your offer, put the picture of your opt in offer up, and link to your squeeze page so your readers can opt in.

Copy and paste the offer and put it at the end of your book too. Here's an example of one of mine:

Natural Hair Checklist & Journal [FREE]

Our printable checklist provides you with a list of everything you'll need to begin your natural hair journey.

Take it with you on the go, it can be downloaded on any device.

Click Here For Access

As an added **BONUS** you'll receive our **Natural Hair Journey Journal**. A digital journal where you can track your experiences of growth, recipes, and more.

The journal is exclusive for customers of our natural hair books, you can access it at the **end of this book!**

Going Beyond Your Book

If you have an author website, make sure you have opt in forms on the sidebars and underneath each page or blog post.

Also, test your conversions to increase opt ins; you can do this by using squeeze pages, splash pages, pop ups, or simply changing your offer or the description, and image of your offer.

Get Highest Conversions

In order to get higher conversions, you'll have to test to see what works best. This means learning about copywriting, designing, or outsourcing the whole thing.

Sometimes the play on words can increase an opt in. For example: using "grab your free report" may convert less than "grab my free report". Because you're using the word "my", prospects my see it as something more exclusive which will most likely lead them to opt in.

Test the following for your opt in offer:

- colors

- headlines

- size of text

- words used in offer

- image of the offer

- the offer itself

- etc.

Another way to get feedback from your offer to is see how much your subscribers enjoyed it; ask your subscribers if they enjoyed the offer in a follow up email.

Ask subscribers if there's any way you can improve the offer and ask them if they have any questions. You should get some emails back letting you know the impact the offer had.

The Takeaway

All in all, you have your work cut out for you. Now I want you to start creating your landing page. After your offer is completed; place it in the front of your book(s), right after the title page.

Then place the offer in the back of your book(s) right after the conclusion.

As I mentioned, if you're discussing anything related to your opt in offer throughout your book, link to your landing page. Don't just mention it randomly.

Keep in mind that you may have to create more than one opt in offer if you have books that are completely unrelated. Don't put up opt in offers that are unrelated to what the book is about. This will only confuse the reader, and you're not likely to get a targeted group of subscribers this way.

Have a Bunch Of Books on Different Topics

Your best bet is to make an offer that is a free books giveaway. So when you have a new book, you can send it to your readers, no matter the subject. Some people just like to get stuff for free.

This strategy is better than nothing, but the best way to build the backend is to have related books so you can sell your readers more related books and set up your email auto responders accordingly.

So even if you need time to start creating some related books, that's fine. Right now just put opt the "free books" opt in offer. This is better than nothing. You need to start collecting emails today; even if they're not targeted.

Overall

So, right now **get your opt in offer created** and place it in the front and back of your books. You need to start working on this now so you can so you can have something in place.

Every day you wait, you're missing out on tons of leads, fans, and back end money from your books. So it doesn't matter what you have to put off today, clear your schedule and get your landing page and offer created.

In the next chapter we're going to go into how to choose an affiliate product or a product.

Chapter 3: Choosing Affiliate Offer or Product

Choosing the right product for your audience is not necessarily easy, but it's simple. You need to keep in mind that this is not a get rich quick scheme and you truly want to provide value to your audience and build a relationship with them via email marketing so they begin to trust you.

So make sure you do your due diligence if you're going to create your own product; and also make sure its valuable; and that your readers will get a lot out of it. If you plan on promoting an affiliate product make sure it's a quality product.

If you can, actually purchase the product and go through it so you can give a thorough review before sending it out to your email list.

If your readers see that you are recommending high quality products, they'll be more prone to trusting you and may purchase other things from you in the future.

Creating Your Own Product

Creating your own product can be a long drawn out process if you don't know what you're doing; but if you have the right resources and tools the process can be pretty simple.

You can create a WordPress site where you're able to host your product on your own domain. You can use free tools and plug-ins such as S2member in order to set up a payment gateway which only allows certain people to see certain content on that particular website.

If you never set up a website before, you can do so by going to http://www.ArgenaOlivis.com/website/for a tutorial on how to set up a website from scratch. But before setting up your website and hosting your own domain name you're going to need to create content for your information product.

There is a ton of different information products you can create. You can create an e-book out of a PDF, video courses, MP3s, and any other form of digital media that can be delivered straight to the consumer after purchase.

Video Creation

You can create videos by recording yourself or you can record your screen depending on what type of course you're going to be delivering. When recording yourself the videos are usually more personal and you're usually explaining a certain concept.

But if it's an information product where you want to show your students your computer screen in order to walk them through exactly how to do something; you can use a screen recording tool.

There are many different options for recording your computer screen; many are free. My favorite one to use is Screen-Cast-O-Matic, but there's also one called Audacity for PC users. These screen recording tools are usually very low-priced or or are free to use so that you don't have to worry about paying a lot to get started creating your course.

Jing is also another one that can be used with both Mac and PC. Tools like Jing are great for taking pictures of your screen and capturing different things that you're trying to explain.

You may want to capture your screen to further explain things in a PDF or e-book that you're selling. What you want to do is create your videos and store them in a place where no one can access them on the Internet for free.

There are services you can use to store your videos and put them into your website. Make sure that with any books or products that you create, you keep them stored in more than one place.

Don't leave all your information in one place for security reasons. One storage space that I was looking into is called Amazon S3. The thing here is when you want to create your own information product you have to have somewhere to store your information so no one else can have access to those videos or your e-book without paying for your content.

So make sure whatever service that you choose can be secured so not anyone can access your videos; only members of that particular product will be able to see the videos that you created for them.

Besides setting up a membership site using a free plugin service called S2Member, and making sure your videos are stored in your Wordpress website and not just anyone has access to them; you should be pretty much good to go.

All you have to do is organize your course the way you want it and you'll be able to set up a buy button where people can purchase your product. If you really don't like the idea of doing all this work you can either outsource it, or you can use a service called Udemy.com, they offer a free way to create courses.

All you'd have to do is become an Udemy instructor and you can basically host your course there for free. They do have to approve your course, but it's a great way to get started if you're a beginner.

You also get to connect with different instructors. The only thing that some people don't like about Udemy is that when you start with them they make you sign a contract where they have the rights to put your course on sale at any time.

But they also give you option to give out coupons or offer your course for free to certain people by creating coupons. This system is very simple and easy-to-use the system is very organized and they allow you to upload lectures and different downloads for your course.

In Udemy you can also post announcements and things like that. You'll also get the upside of their traffic that's already on their site and their students that they already have.

Just like Amazon, you can utilize their traffic and get upside of connecting with more people and finding more readers, and in turn creating the back end for your books.

Creating MP3s

You also have the option of creating MP3s for your readers in order to sell to them on the back end. Similar to creating an audiobook, MP3s can be something that your audience may want; they may be tired of reading and want to listen to something.

The audiobook market is definitely booming and is only getting larger. You don't necessarily have to create an audiobook; you could also create MP3s that have supplemental PDFs and images that explain the different techniques that you're teaching.

Of course, most of this only applies to nonfiction authors, but if you get creative you never know what may work for your audience on the back end. You can create MP3s by using services such as SoundCloud; or maybe even create an Mp3 using an app on your phone that you can record something and send to your email, then in turn upload it to your membership site and sell access to your audience.

Internet Marketing Strategies

You can meet people in the internet marketing space and other authors and they can help you to promote your product, if it's a very good product. So make sure you provide a lot of value in the product, and that what you are creating actually helps people get results.

You could also put your product on affiliate channels such as Jvzoo and Clickbank, these affiliate networks will can help you get more affiliates. Also, make sure you're always connecting with other authors and the people in your niche.

Creating eBooks

eBooks are another type of information product that you can create. They're fairly easy to make. Creating an eBook is similar to creating a Kindle book, but you just export as PDF and make sure no one will have access to it, unless they are a part of your site or have purchased it through you.

So if you do decide to create an eBook outside of Kindle for the back end, think about it being related to the eBook that your reader already purchased.

Also think about if your one e-book gets a lot of traction, you can convert the readers to buy your eBooks directly from your website and cut out the middleman which is Amazon.

This is a good strategy to make more money on the back end. You could have one series on Amazon that is very popular. Make sure to really get a lot of reviews for that particular kindle.

After getting new customers on your email list, introduce them to your other eBooks which they can only purchase from your site; and then you cut Amazon out so they don't take any of your royalties which gives you a higher margin; hence, building the back end.

Your readers will still be able to read your work on a Kindle device. Most smart phones and devices ask how you want to open a particular file; if they are on a Kindle or have the Kindle app, they should be able to read the eBook through their device.

There are many strategies you can use to make more money on the back end, you just have to be creative.

Upselling Affiliate Products

Finding affiliate products is one of the easier things to do; not only do you not have to create the product, it is easy to find products in almost any niche. The first thing you want to make sure of is that the product is relevant to whatever your book is about.

This is another thing that might be more for nonfiction authors. So what you want to do is find big affiliate sites that are reputable and start searching for products that are perfect for your audience.

The best way to be a great affiliate marketer is to actually test out the products. You can give the best testimonials when you actually use the products. It's important to create trust, and you want to make sure to recommend products that are top notch.

You don't want to put your reputation in jeopardy. A few dollars is not worth a lifetime customer. You don't necessarily have to use the product, although that will be nice, but I do recommend that you do your research on the product to make sure that people were actually getting results with it.

The best sites to find affiliate products are Clickbank, JVzoo, Share-a-sale, and Commission Junction. There are tons of sites that offer affiliate programs, but you just want to make sure that the one you choose pays a good amount and it's something you can stand by; and is relevant to your audience.

The best way to sell an affiliate product is through your email list. But you can also link to offers on your website. There are certain guidelines to use when promoting an affiliate offer; make sure that other people are having success with it, make sure that other people are getting results with it, make sure that it'll pay you a decent amount of money for the promotions are going to be doing.

Make sure that the sales page is decent in that it converts well. The great thing about having an email list is that you can test out different things to see what works. Some affiliates even offer email templates that you can use in order to promote the product your list.

Some affiliate products have great support for their affiliates. Some actually offer training on how to sell the product. So make sure when choosing an affiliate product that it's relevant and that you have great support from the owner of the product.

More Affiliate Marketing Tips

I love reading, so when I do; the one thing I appreciate is when the author gives me information that I can use and put into action right now. The following are actionable items that you can do right away to increase your income for the back end of your kindle books.

Buy Domain Name

For your bigger affiliate products you'll be promoting, consider buying a domain name for the affiliate offer. You can then set it up so when people type that domain name in it'll go straight to the affiliate product.

Set this up by going into the control panel of where you purchased your domain name and have it forwarded. This means, when people type the domain name into their browser or click on it, it'll go right over to the affiliate offer.

Domain names are not just for websites, be creative and use them for your products and affiliate offers to increase conversions. This is also a good way to mask your domain name, just in case you don't want clicks to the product to be tracked.

It also looks more professional. I use Godaddy to host all my domain names, and the process is pretty simple there. Plus, I love how you can get promo codes when buying new domains to get them for super cheap.

If you're not able to buy domain names for some reason, you can always use a WordPress plugin called Pretty Link. It has the same effect, but the difference is; the link will start with the beginning of the domain name for your website and then you can create any link you want without having to create a new page for your site.

In Pretty Link, you can set it up so the link is "no follow" so you don't have to worry about the search engines picking it up or any algorithm online picking it up. In this plugin, you simply type in the link that you want prospects to be forwarded to and then choose the link extension.

Review the Affiliate Product

Reviewing the affiliate product will definitely increase your conversions. Let your readers know the results you've gotten by using the product personally. You can do your review through video or written on your website or email.

Also, if at all possible, walk them through the product to show them what they'll be receiving and what it looks like, features, etc. It's best if they see you actually own the product, they may not fully trust you right now so give them a reason to.

It's not easy to build trust online, so make it so that they don't have any question in their mind that they'll be getting value for what they pay for.

Prove to your readers that the product is currently working or has worked for you in the past. You can also create tutorials around the product to create more trust and authority for the product.

Create a Bonus

Make it clear to your audience that it is an affiliate link. Also let them know if they purchase the product through your affiliate link that they'll receive something of value for free.

Create a bonus that related directly to the product and give it away to those that purchase the product through your affiliate link.

To automate this, set up a different email address for your product and when a customer emails their receipt as proof of purchase, have a vacation email that delivers the product to them automatically.

Although this may not be the most secure way, it'll still work. Don't worry about people stealing, it's free anyways. And what goes around, comes around.

The Takeaway

All in all, having a valuable product on the back end ensures that you're truly building the back end of your kindle business.

Going through the trouble of setting all of this up also shows that you're serious about your business and adding value to your readers.

You can be as creative as you like in choosing products to promote and or create. Not all readers will buy, but most will appreciate all the value you've given them. Keep creating and or looking for the perfect affiliate products for your audience. Take out all the hard guess work for them and really sell to them what you feel will help them out.

Chapter 4: Setting Up Auto responders

In order to set up a real business you going to need to set up auto responders so you don't have to manually email your list whenever you have something new to say.

Most email marketing software comes with features that allow you to set up auto responders. If you're using Aweber you can check out my tutorial on how to set up auto responders if you're a beginner. Visit ArgenaOlivis.com/email-marketing-101

Your First Email

The first email that your readers will receive is an email welcoming them to your list and that has your opt in offer in it. This email is automatically sent out to any new subscriber on your list.

All you have to do is place the first email that they'll receive into your auto responder and when they subscribe, they'll automatically get the gift that they were opting in for. So no matter what you're giving away, make sure you have a link to your download, MP3, video, or whatever you're giving your new subscribers for free.

Also this email should consistent with what the reader should suspect in the future when hearing from you. Make your welcome email as personal as you can. And in the subject line, put something related to the free gift that they receiving.

For example: My first email usually begins with:

"Congratulations! Download your _____ (insert free gift name)".

In order to set up your first email, you must first create a new list in your email software. After creating the list, create the first email for that list; make sure the email will be sent out automatically when someone confirms their subscription.

Leveraging The Thank you page

After setting up your first email you want to make sure that your thank you page is set up too. Your thank you page is something that you really want to take advantage of because it's the first thing that people see when they subscribe to your list.

A thank you page basically thanks the new subscriber for opting in. It's the page where can tell readers what to expect in future emails. On this page you can do a lot. You can offer an affiliate product or your own products at a sale price since new subscribers won't be seeing this page again.

When you do offer an affiliate product or your product on this page, it warms your potential subscribers and long-term readers up for future promotions. It's great for people to know that this is not going to be a list were they'll just getting free stuff all the time.

I've used this method and I've got affiliate sales through my thank you page. So in the beginning you just want to basically thank them for subscribing to your list. You have the option to link to a blog post that is very popular if you have a blog.

You also have the option to tell them what to expect; such as the first email from you, what the email will look like when they go to claim their free gift, when the email will arrive, etc.

After letting the new subscriber know what to expect; you can have them scroll down and offer a product to them. The product can be offered at a discounted rate that the subscriber won't see again, or you can just let them know that you've used the product and give a link to a free video or free download so you can take them over to sales page.

The Second Email

The second email will be set up to go out when you want it to. This can be two days after the first message or three days after the first message it depends on how often you want to keep in contact with your list.

I recommend sending an email every two days, but not every single day. You don't want to wear out your list. You really to provide value every time that you actually email them. You don't have to set up auto responders for the whole year. You can set them up as you create new content.

You can also send broadcast emails after your auto responder is finished to a certain portion of your list. You can be strategic when sending out broadcast messages versus auto responders.

For example: You can have Monday through Friday be the only days that you send auto responder messages, and you can have it so that broadcast messages are only sent on the weekends.

Being strategic to when emailing your list will ensure that subscribers are not getting more than one email from you on that day. You also have the option to email people that have gone through your auto responder sequence already.

Email marketing software is very technical and you can do a lot with it. You can even set up the time that the email goes out. So for your second email you may want to send them an offer. If you do decide to promote an offer to your list, you can set it up so you can tell if someone has purchased item or not.

You can do all this fancy stuff through most email marketing software. The great thing about this is if someone clicks on the link to get on a new list this means that this is a list of people that want to hear more about what you have.

So create a new list every time you're offering something for people to buy or something that you want a separate list for; such as groups, different books, and interests in particular subjects.

Be strategic about separating your lists. We will get more into segmentation in the next chapter. Your second email can also be filled with content, there so many options of what you can send your list.

It is probably best to send your list content rather than an offer but it depends on what your goal is with your list. If you really want to blow them away before offering them something to buy; there's nothing wrong with that.

You can create content that is exclusive for your list and send them over to your content. This could be on your blog or it can be a YouTube video that is unlisted. Just as long as you're sending content that will help them solve a problem or entertain them.

If they're just discovering you as an author, there's a chance that they haven't watched any of your YouTube videos. It's also a chance that they haven't looked to all your blog posts; so make sure that you are sharing your best content with them.

The best thing about this is that you already have content created for them. Subscribers would also like to know that they are getting exclusive content. So if you want to just create a video or something that's only for your list then they'll feel more special.

Make sure to mention in the email that it's a "subscriber only" email. A lot of this may pertain to nonfiction authors, but fiction authors can take advantage of this too. You just have to be more creative.

Fiction Authors

When it comes to email marketing, the idea here is to keep the reader engaged. You can do behind the scenes of the characters, you can offer your list free books, and you can also create merchandise around your particular characters or book title.

Create things like bookmarks and T-shirts. Be creative and sell different things from the book; for example: use quotes that a character with say. Really make a business and brand around the different characters in the book and what's in the book.

You just have to be creative and really think about what you would want if you were in your reader shoes: Would you want to learn more about the characters? Buy different merchandise with quotes from the characters on it?

Build a fan base around your book and your characters. Auto responders can consist of different product offers and different behind the scenes things that fans will enjoy. Also let your list of fans know when the next book is coming out. Make sure you use the preorder function and Amazon Kindle.

Keep your fans updated on what you're up to, and really connect with them think about what they're into. Try to put things in front of them that will allow them to trust you more and will engage them even more in the book and in the content in the book.

The Take Away

All in all, make sure you put yourself in your subscriber's shoes. Make sure that you're sending them relevant content, and things that they will enjoy. Make it so that they are excited to see an email from you.

Create value and set up auto responders so you can focus on other things like building your back end for other books. You really have to treat this as a business if you want to build your back end.

There's a lot to do and it's a lot of action to take but it will be worth it in the end. So before sending out anything, ask yourself "how would I feel if I got this email in my inbox."

If you can help people they will appreciate you and they will repay you either monetarily or by leaving you reviews. By just being a fan that is getting all this valuable content for free, when they do have the money you'll be the first place they'll go.

So make sure to get your auto responders set up, so you can engage with people and see what people really want in order to serve them better. The thing that you should be focusing on is writing, finding more ways to get subscribers, and selling more books.

You should be worried about marketing you shouldn't be worried about manually sending out emails. Create systems so that if you can't be in your business daily; you have everything set up so that you won't have to worry. The great thing about books are they can be very passive, so make your whole business passive so you're able to serve more people.

Chapter 5: Separate Lists/Segmentation

Eventually you want to get more advanced in your email marketing campaigns. You want to set up different lists in order to know who your buyers are and who your general audience is. Creating a list of buyers will allow you to see what subscribers are interested in, and what subscribers do not react to.

If the product that you put out is quality and your customers get results from it; they'll want to know more about other offers that you have.

Automation

In most email software, I know this happens in Aweber, you can set up a list automation. This is when a subscriber subscribes to one list, they get taken off another list at the same time.

For example: if you have a general list about Internet marketing and you want to get more specific on who's interested in email marketing. You would create a new list and send an email to your current list, the email would be an opt in offer to get on the email marketing list. Once they subscribe to your email marketing list, they'll be taken your general internet marketing list.

You could also have different products that your general list may be interested in; you want to make a list of subscribers that are interested in that specific product. So instead of keep emailing your general list about the product, email your general list a link to another opt in offer and set up an automation rule where they'll be put on a new list.

Make sure when separating your lists that they're very specific; so you'll know what to send each list. Once you create a lot of lists, it can get kind of complicated; so in the beginning just make sure that you name your list things that you will remember later on.

So the idea here is to create one list per related topic or book. So if you have a series of books, you want all those people on one list. If you have another book that's in a completely different niche, you want to create a separate list which means you may want to create a separate Opt in offer in order to get people to subscribe.

Creating a List of Buyers

This is a technique I use in the niches that I'm very serious about. I create a list of buyers so I know that these people actually invested in my book. The only way you can really do this is to have your opt in offer at the very end.

But you still don't want to miss out on those emails from prospects that may not buy the book but have opted in through the preview or "look inside" feature that Amazon offers. In order to do this you want to have two opt in offers: one general offer that is put at the front of your books, this offer can also be put on your website and in other places too.

You want to have a second opt in offer that you put at the end of your book. With this offer, tell readers in advance that "if you want to get this offer you have to scroll down to the bottom of the book, it's only for customers" of that particular book. Make this very clear to your readers.

Highlight the words when explaining that they need to scroll down to the end of the book to get the second opt in offer. So what you do here is create two separate lists; one with just the general opt in offer and one with both offers. The one with both offers is put at end of the book.

As far as free days go make sure to take your second offer out the end of book. You specifically want to build a list of buyers. Customers that you know have purchased the book. Also make sure that this is something that people will scroll to the end of the book to opt in for. So make both offers irresistible.

I see low numbers of people that opt in at the end of the book; but at least I have actual buyers that I know invested in my product. This makes the second sell so much easier if the product they purchased from me was valuable.

So make sure that the offer is valuable, and that it's something people really want. It takes a while to build two opt in offers but it's definitely worth it in order to build a list of buyers. Make sure to keep testing your opt in offers often; tweak it and see if anything increases number of people subscribing at the end of the book and getting on the list of buyers.

The Take Away

Overall you want to be very serious in your email marketing efforts. Yes, you want to keep things simple but you also want to create different lists in order to truly connect with people on a deeper level.

The more targeted your list is, the easier it will be to create content and create auto responders. Knowing that you have a list of buyers is gold. These subscribers are ten times more likely to buy something else from you if they see that your book was good.

All in all make sure you use separate lists and segmentation in order to increase conversions and truly create assets in your business.

Chapter 6: Keep Readers Engaged

You really want to keep your readers. You don't want them to just read your book and then go on to the next book. If you don't engage your readers, there's other authors that are taking their Kindle business seriously that will take your readers away. So you want to make sure that you're on top of things and that you're actually creating a business in a loyal fan base.

I do believe in abundance, and that there's enough room for everyone; but if you can engage your readers better than the next author, you can build long term relationships and a profitable business.

Send Relevant Content

Make sure that whatever you send your list is actually relevant. If you create a list of people that were interested in your book, that shouldn't be a problem. But if you have a general list of people you give random free books to, don't expect them to be as engaged as someone who opted in because they liked your particular book in that particular niche.

Don't feel bad when people unsubscribe from your list, this only means that they may have a different interest at the time and or are no longer interested in that particular subject. If a lot of people are unsubscribing because of a particular message, just make sure that you step up your game and actually think about if you would want the message you sent in your inbox.

In most email marketing software you can set it up so that you can look at the analytics of subscribes and unsubscribes. It's very advanced, you can see who unsubscribed after what message was sent. So whatever your opt in offer is, make sure that your auto responders are similar to it. Make sure that you stick to the subject.

Free or Sales on Books

When you have free books, do not try to hide that from your audience. When your audience gets bigger, you'll be able to launch a book once it on sale at $.99, you can send it to your audience and get a lot of downloads and reviews for that book on the particular launch date.

So when you have free books, make sure send the free book to your audience so they can download it. Your list should be treated very well, so if you have a free book make sure to share it with them.

They will appreciate you and some may buy your other books if they haven't yet. By you having a giving heart, and not a heart of scarcity; your subscribers will find value on being on your list and open your emails if they know that you may **Have sales your books.**

You can have different sales for holidays, just because, or when you're partnering with different authors. So if your books are usually priced at $2.99 or $3.99, you want to have them also for $0.99 and let your audience know that your books are on sale.

Social Media

Social media is not just a way to promote your books is also a way to keep your readers engaged. Social media can be used to answer reader questions, reach out to other authors, build your email list, and give out tips related to your topic.

By having a group or social media presence, you're showing that you're an active author and that you really care about your craft. Social media is also a great place to post when you have free books or sales on your books; it can increase the amount of downloads you get for your book, which in turn will get more people on your list and get you more readers.

You can create profiles on popular sites such as Facebook, Twitter, Pinterest, and LinkedIn. Facebook is definitely the most popular form of social media that authors are using. You can also create Facebook ads in order to get more people to your books or to your list.

Also consider joining or creating a Facebook group where you can interact with your readers or give them further attention. This is a great way to sell more of your books. It's also way to sell more of other products you offer.

So having other things outside of your books like a Facebook group can definitely increase the back end of your Kindle business. The more the readers get to know and trust you, the more that you'll make. So building a community of loyal readers and customers online is definitely something that you want to focus on. Social media can do that for you.

Focus

Don't go on Twitter, Facebook, Pinterest, and LinkedIn all at the same time. Pick one social media platform and dominate it before moving on to another. Also don't let social media come in the way of your writing.

What you should be focusing on is writing and building

your back end, and your email list. But social media is definitely another way and another channel to get more readers on your email list. So make sure to master one of these skills.

Pick the platform that may be best for your particular readers you can do that by doing some more research on where your readers are hanging out. It can also vary by niche, if your readers are very visual they may enjoy platforms like Facebook and Pinterest. But if they're more professional and business minded, they may be on platforms like Linked In and Twitter.

Create a Website

If you haven't yet, make sure to create a website around your book series. This will give readers a hub where they can go in learn more about your business. It doesn't have to be a huge website, but you do need to have one in order to look more professional if you want a real business.

I usually put a link to my website right under the title of my book. This allows people looking at the preview to see that I do more than just write books; that I actually have a presence online. And they can get access to some of my tutorials or some of my content and see that I have expertise in what I write about.

You don't have to necessarily write a bunch of blog posts; you can also just have a website that is focused on the series of your books. Make sure you have an opt in offer and a place where readers can contact you.

Make sure to put a contact me form up when your website, just in case readers are other authors want to reach out to you.

All in all, you just need a small website that can help you capture more leads via email marketing. Your website can help engage more readers by providing them with more content or more information about you and your books series.

The Takeaway

When going into this, you want to make sure you're thinking of ways to add value to your readers. So take their feedback, and really update your books as you go along. All feedback is not going to be relevant, but you do want to see it through the readers' eyes.

By keeping readers engaged and updating your content by telling them what's new and updating them on any new books coming out; you create a fan base that is loyal more quickly.

So by keeping in touch with them through your website and through social media by telling them there are sales on books and by sending them relevant content you're able to create a community that's engaged in that you can sell to later on.

As people see that you're creating a fan base and a see that you're providing value to your readers; they'll most likely want to be a part of the community and it will be a snowball effect.

So just make sure you're thinking of new ways you can add value to your readers in creating new products and or getting affiliate products were you can help them on the larger scale. I know you'll do well because if you're reading this book you obviously want to serve your audience.

Chapter 7: Building A Real Business

It's simple to make a profit from Amazon's platform. Amazon itself has a lot of traffic and if you use the right keywords it's easy to sell a book where you're are making a profit of two dollars to six dollars.

But the point of building the back end is to have your own platform. So you don't have to rely on Amazon's traffic just in case something happens. So what you have to do is actually build a real business; just in case you decide that you want to do something else later on.

A real business allows you to have passive income while you're vacationing, allows you to have control, and allows you to focus on the things that you want and be more creative. You know you're running a real business when you have a community of fans that are excited to purchase from you.

You also know when you're running a real business when you can step outside the business and everything keeps going in income keeps coming in. A real business is something that you will be able to sell in the future, it's something that you look at as an investment and for creating wealth.

I know this book is called Kindle Publishing Back End, but eventually you may want to publish on other platforms. You may want to publish in other languages. You may want to create paperback books for your business and also audiobooks.

The great thing about being an independent author is that you can have all rights to different territories and you can have separate products for just one book. So let's get into some things that will help take your business forward.

Daily routine

Create a daily routine for which will work on your Kindle business. You have to stay organized in order to take your business to next love level. Your daily routine should ideally consist of things that will move your business forward.

This can consist of working on auto responders, creating paperback books for your kindle books, creating audiobooks, emailing your list, promoting your books, or getting interviewed or doing an interview to market your book. You also may want to do some speaking engagements in order to truly get your name out there. It all depends on the system you build for your business and what your marketing plan is.

A lot of entrepreneurs also talk about doing a morning routine; this is where you do things like exercise, work on your personal development, work on your motivation, read affirmations, journal, and anything that is not necessarily a practical task but something that will get your mindset right.

Make sure you also have a morning routine, even if you're not a morning person you may want to do this in order to get your mind right. They stated that success is 20% execution in 80% mindset. So if your mindset is not right, you're not going to believe in yourself, you're not going to build a real business, you're just going to let your mind keep you away from what you really want.

You going to talk yourself out of things that will move

your business forward daily. If you don't work on your mindset then there's no way you're going to be running a real business. Don't take motivation and personal development lightly.

Always be reading books and listening to podcasts and different things that will really motivate you so you could see the reasons why you actually want this. If you don't know why you're doing this, you're not going to act on it daily.

If you don't really know why you you're doing this thing, there's no point of really doing it if you're just out to make money because that will not last; that means you're treating this like a get rich quick scheme.

And if you treat kindle like a get rich quick scheme, then your books are not going to do well in perform over time. You're just going to earn enough but you're never going to earn a full-time income.

Put it in your mindset that you're running a full-time business. Make sure you have your taxes together, and make sure that you have set hours for your business; maybe five hours a day or four hours a day depending on what you're working on.

So use a planner or some type of scheduler in order to set up a daily routine that is most productive for you and your lifestyle. You do have enough time in the day, don't tell yourself that you don't.

If you're saying you don't have enough time, that's just an excuse. Really think about what your daily routine should be. It could consists of tasks such as: editing your books, updating your books, updating keywords, getting more reviews, scheduling free promos, etc. Just see what needs done for the week and put it in your planner, write it down.

When you write it down is it is more real. Don't allow distractions to take you away from your daily routine, don't go to sleep until everything on your list is crossed out. Soon you'll find yourself always working on your business and always knowing exactly what you need to do for the day. So select the perfect daily routine for yourself and get started.

Focus

You really have to focus if you want to build a real business. I had to take out three months where all I worked on was my Kindle business. This wasn't easy because I have a lot of other income streams that I'm working on online.

But I had to put those projects aside because I really felt like if I focused on one thing that I can make it really great. As a result my income dramatically increased for Kindle, Createspace, and ACX.

And during this time I was working on everything in my Kindle business and getting everything set up in process, so that I can eventually hand some things over to a virtual assistant (VA). Focus is amazing and focus with action is success.

So if you really want to hit your goals then you need to focus on just Kindle. Focusing on one project will allow you to get ahead in hit goals that we wouldn't be able to otherwise. If you're always worried about another platform then you're going to get overwhelmed and not really understand what direction you're going in.

So instead of trying to juggle everything, say "okay, for three months I'm just going to focus on one business."

You'll be happy you did. Because your income will increase, you will hit goals, and have a steady income coming in while you create other streams of income online if that's what you choose to do.

If you just want to be a full-time author and nothing else, then that's great because you know what you want to do and you know why you want to do it. Lots of people jump around and they really don't understand why they're not getting the results they want.

So being actual full-time author and only focusing on writing for the rest your life is definitely a plan. Just as long as you're building your email list and you're not only on Amazon's platform. But definitely focus on what you can improve in your Kindle business and focus on just Kindle for at least three months so you can get off the ground and make a steady income monthly.

Entrepreneurs are always looking at different things and wanting to jump around, but it really hurts us in the end. There's only so many things we can do in a day, and we really need to focus in order to move things forward.

If you focus on Kindle, make a promise to yourself to only focus on it until you're making a certain dollar amount; and if you move on to something else, that's great too. And then while you're creating another income stream you'll still have your Kindle income coming in where you can maintain it once a week if you have the best system in place; such as a team of VA's.

So the great thing about this is, if you go full time you can create your own schedule. Realize how important focus is. Focus will really help you. So in order to build a real business make sure to focus at all times.

When to Write

The best time to write is when you first wake up. I usually write after I do my morning routine. I don't write "as soon" as I wake up; I don't open my laptop until I finish my morning routine. After that, I'm ready to start writing.

Write whenever you have time, maybe the morning won't work for you; maybe you're not full-time yet, so write when you have time. But most people like to write in the morning because their brain is still fresh and you don't have the worries throughout the day to worry about while you're writing and that can interrupt your creative process.

Make sure you have goals, such as, how many pages you want to write a day or how many words that you want to write a day. You can keep track of this in your schedule or calendar. Or if you just want to write for a specific amount of time, like an hour day.

I usually go by time; I write for an hour day. I used to actually physically type out my books but recently I've been using an application from my iPhone called Dragon, this is where I just speak and I say what I want to say; then save it and send it to my email. Then I paste it into a word document.

This allows for more productivity because I think faster than I can write. I found myself with my wrist hurting and in uncomfortable positions from writing too much and typing too much. So if I have a book to write, I'm actually reading it and then the Dragon app translates it so that you don't have to worry about typing.

This may be weird at first but it really works and you should really try it out. It's a free app at the moment. The only thing about the app is that most of the time you have to go in and edit your work and maybe send it to a professional editor.

But besides that, if you know what you're talking about, it can be a breeze. Just try to talk clearly and there's different commands you can voice in the app that puts in punctuation and indentations and things like that.

So make sure you're writing and timing your writing or writing until you get a certain word count done for the day. If you want to make writing your career and your full-time occupation then make sure you're serious about writing consistently; this means every single day.

When To Promote

Real authors actually promote their books. There are many places to promote. We already talked a little about social media in chapter 6; we talked about focusing on one channel that brings you the most results.

So the best time to promote is daily. Amazon has already done promotions for your books, but you still want to promote books to the readers you already have. So make sure that at the end of your books you're linking to different books that you've already written that are similar to books that the customers are reading at the time.

Also promote when you have a Kindle countdown deal or a five day free promotion. Make sure to promote your book in different groups and wherever your choice of social media is. There's other ways to market a book, such as having YouTube videos, having links to your books on your website, or even having a signature on your emails that says check out my book.

You can get very creative with your promotions just see

what's working best and keep doing that. There's no need to go on platforms that don't bring in any new readers. Really try to track where most of your readers are coming from.

So promote your book when you're getting interviewed on a podcast, when you're at a networking meeting, or anytime you see fit. The best times to market productively are when you're not feeling creative enough to write; these are the perfect times to promote because usually when you plan book promotions your mind is in a different place.

You're really thinking about how you can get more sales or how you can serve more people instead of thinking about characters and subject matter. So use the time when you are not writing to do your marketing. .

VA's

VA's are virtual assistants. Virtual assistants are can really help you to build a real business. As I'm writing this book, I'm actually about to start implementing VA's into to my Kindle business because I'm making an income where I can afford to do so.

This will in turn allow you to free up more time to work on other projects, or just write

more books. The kind of things that you can have your VA do is: promote your books, format your books, buy covers, update your social media pages, and even write your books depending on if you use ghost writers.

The best place to hire a VA today is oDesk. Because they're able to track things in their work journal so they can take screenshots of the VA's computer while they are working to make sure you're getting your money's worth.

Also oDesk holds your VA accountable; if your VA doesn't do a great job then you're most likely not going to leave them very good feedback. The lowest amount that you could probably pay Vas these days is about three dollars an hour.

Anything less than that is kind of crazy. Three dollars or four dollars an hour is pretty suitable for a VA from the Philippines. People choose Filipino VAs because of the language and culture similarities between them and the US. Also many people from the Philippines are not very entrepreneurial.

They just really want to take on work and work for you in order to provide for their family in most cases. Also a lot of them are very great with computers and different tasks. Make sure to interview potential team members on Skype or something like that and treat them as actual person because they are actual people with actual feelings.

This will free up your time to do other things and invest in other businesses. Depending on what your goals are, you may want to just continue to write more books and get more content out there.

Or you may want to work on another project; it all depends on what your goals are. Just as long as you're focusing on one thing at a time you should be fine. Make sure your VA is well-trained and make sure that you're saving documents.

Make sure that your VA or you are writing SOP's or standard operating procedures so if they ever quit, someone can easily replace them by reading the directions or watching a video in order to see what they're supposed to be doing.

So whatever tasks that you're currently doing, you can create a video by capturing a screen using a tool such as Screen-Cast-O-Matic or Jing. You can capture your screen and record your screen while you're completing different tasks in your business. So in the future you can outsource these tasks to a VA so they'll know what to do on a daily basis. All in all, a honest and loyal VA will be a great addition to your team and into your life in order to create business of freedom.

The Takeaway

All in all, you want to build a real business in order to have a great foundation where your income cannot be wiped out overnight. It will give you security and will give you more peace of mind knowing that you have your books on different platforms and you have an email list just in case something does go down.

Ask yourself how you can create more value for someone else. It's time to start looking at your Kindle business as just more than Kindle and start creating other forms of content too. Really try to do things that you've never done and get out of your comfort zone. Network with other authors and just do things that you never done before and that's when you'll see the most growth in your business.

Your mind will definitely try to stop you because it wants to keep you safe; it doesn't like to see new things. But if you can get through that and you truly work on your mindset and set up a daily routine for yourself, you're already ahead of most authors. I know you'll do well since you got to the end of this book that means that you're serious and you're really trying to take your business to the next level.

Conclusion

Another thanks for investing in this book and getting to the end. Remember that all of this information means nothing without action. Go out there and implement the strategies in this book and get yourself some results!

If you got anything that you can use out of this book that will make a difference in your Kindle business, please review this book on Amazon. As you know, reviews help more readers to find the book. It also gives me feedback on how I can improve the book. Pay it forward!

Thank you and good luck!

Preview Of 'Email Marketing Machine'

Chapter 1: Establishing Your Target Market

How well do you know your customer? Do you know what they like to do? What their interests are? How you can help them? If not, that's okay we're going to learn all about that.

But first, you need to establish a niche if you haven't already. A niche is a specific topic that you want to focus on. You may already have a website, service, or product that already focuses on a specific topic.

There are some guidelines you need to follow when choosing your niche: profitability, knowledge, likeability, and size.

Profitability

Before you choose a niche, you want to ensure it's profitable. You can find this out by visiting Google.com and typing in your topic and seeing how other people are making money with this niche.

Visit a few of the top websites. If you choose this niche, these will be your competitors. Competition is a good thing, this means there's money to be made.

Don't worry too much about the size of their audience. The one thing that you can do differently is be yourself. Your competitor can never be you, you're original so make sure to use that as an advantage. You shouldn't dwell on what you cannot change.

When you visit their website, see how they're making

money. Do they offer coaching? Do they have a brick in mortar? Services? Their own store or products and courses? Affiliate marketing?

This will be most likely how you will be making money too, so get some ideas and jot them down.

If the site you visit looks like they are making money with just advertising, you may want to stay away from that. Only because you don't want to put all your eggs in one basket.

If they have private ads from different companies, you may be on to something. But it's still too risky.

Do they have products or services in this niche? If they do, there's most likely people making money from it. This means it's profitable.

If you think about going into a niche that doesn't already have products or services, this will not be a smart move.

Internet marketing has been around for years, and if no one has created a product for your niche, then it's most likely not profitable because it doesn't have a big enough audience.

You ultimately want to make a profit and you can't do that with a non-profitable niche.

Other techniques you can use is to see if your niche has products on big sites like Clickbank or Amazon.com.

Use Amazon search to your advantage by seeing if there are at books selling on the topic you're thinking about getting into.

Do this by typing in a keyword and seeing how profitable the book is. You can tell how profitable a book is by the rank. If it's below 100,000 in the paid kindle store, this means it's making some money.

Knowledge

How much knowledge and experience do you have in the niche? You're going to need it.

You can always study a particular niche, but that's going to take a lot of time and be difficult for you.

But if you have the money, you can always outsource content using services such as Odesk, Elance, and Fiverr.

If you truly want to learn more about the niche, consider doing a "journey". This is where you take people through your journey of that niche.

For example: My site Argena Olivis is about my journey to online business success. I'm taking people on a journey and showing them how I'm creating multiple streams of income online.

You can do this with a niche to, but you truly have to be committed to learning a lot and growing over time so your audience can see progress.

You may be thinking that you can't find a niche because you're not necessarily good or passionate about anything in particular. Well, I think there has to be something you like a lot.

Think about how you spend your free time. Do you have any hobbies such as scrap-booking or fixing cars?

There's something you're good at. If you're truly struggling on finding a niche, make sure to ask the people closest to you what they think you're good at and then try to find a profitable niche from there.

If you have a lot of money, and not time. Consider outsourcing your content. This may be expensive, but it's totally worth it if you want to be in that niche.

You can do this by going to places like Fiverr.com, Odesk.com, and Elance.com.

Likeability

You have to like the niche you choose. If you don't like it, you're not going to stick with it and it's not fair to your audience.

You don't have to be passionate about it, but you should at least find it interesting.

It's dangerous getting into a niche you don't believe in or you don't truly like. It will show through your emails and your content.

If you don't truly like it, stay away from it. It's not worth the money if your stomach turns every time you have to create content.

Like I said, you don't have to be passionate, but you should come from a place of wanting to help others.

Size

Make sure you choose a niche that is not too small or too broad.

Small niches can be great because you have a very specific target market. But you have to look at it from a profitability stand point too. Don't niche down so far that you're only talking to 20 people.

Don't have your niche so big that you're targeting everybody. This is a mistake. You can't please everyone so don't even try.

This will put a hindrance on building relationships, you can't build relationships through email if you're targeting every type of person.

Being able to stand out from the crowd also comes into play. You want to make sure you stand out and can differentiate yourself from the millions of business owners trying to make money online.

Example: You shouldn't create a market on general weight loss for everyone. Niche down and create a site for weight loss for women. Niche down even further and create a site for weight loss for women in college.

I wouldn't niche down any further than that. But this would be a good target market. Do you get my drift? You want to know who you're target market is so you can actually find them and help them out.

This comes back to knowledge and experience, what do you know? How can you being who you are and where you are be an advantage? Use that info to create your target market if it fits the guidelines.

The Take Away

Please do not skip this step if you don't already have a target market. Without having a specific target market you won't know who to advertise to and who to create emails for.

Know your target market and what stage they're at in life. Are they a beginner or more advanced or anywhere in between?

Once you know who to market to, your life becomes easier and you're able to help other people solve their problems and make money doing it.

If you already have a target market that's great. If not, go through these steps and decide on one. You can always change it later, but for now you want to get started.

I want you to get results from this book. So decide on your target, take action.

Check Out My Other Books

Below you'll find some of my other popular books that are popular on Amazon and Kindle as well. Simply search Amazon to check them out. Alternatively, you can visit my author page on Amazon to see other work done by me.

Email Marketing Machine: Build Relationships Get Traffic and Make Money Online

Make Money Online Fast: Step By Step Instructions On How To Work From Home Using Proven Internet Marketing Strategies

Information Products 101: How To Create And Make Money With Information

Affiliate Marketing 101: How To Make Money With Other People's Products

Online Business Mindset: Confidence Building And Persoanl Development For Internet Marketers

Fulfillment By Amazon For Beginners: Step By Step Instructions On How To Make An Income With FBA

BONUS! Grab My FREE CreateSpace Book Creation Course and ACX Audiobook Creation Course

Get more exposure to your Kindle books by creating paperback books, this means more sales, more authority and leads for the back end of your business!

www.argenaolivis.com/createspaceandaudiobook

As an added bonus, you'll get my ACX Audiobook Creation Course where you'll discover how **to get an audiobook created for FREE!**